Pennies from Heaven

By Koedi Nealy

So much love,
the penny girl!
12·7·2020
kgnealy

Halo
PUBLISHING
INTERNATIONAL

ISBN: 978-1-61244-933-3
LCCN: 2020921488

Halo Publishing International, LLC
8000 W Interstate 10, Suite 600
San Antonio, Texas 78230
www.halopublishing.com

Printed and bound in the United States

I dedicate *"Pennies from Heaven"*
to my mom and dad, Levi and Kristi Nealy.
You have always been my number one supporters!
Thank you for encouraging my life's mission,
guiding me to pursue Christ, and for pushing
me to dream bigger. Because of you,
I am who I am today. I love you, Koedi.

For as long as she could remember, Gracie loved three things: Jesus, pennies and ice cream. She was almost eight years old. That was a long time to love something.

One night after dinner, Gracie told her family, "I think Jesus wants me to help others."

Her daddy replied, "That is great, Gracie. I am sure you will find the perfect way."

Mommy said, "Aw, that's my sweet girl."

"He wants all of us to help others." Her big brother chimed in.

The next morning was shopping day. Gracie loved grocery shopping because she could pick new ice cream flavors. Walking to the car, Gracie spotted a shiny new penny. She was sure someone would pick it up before she got to it.

People never picked up the old damaged ones. This one winked and sparkled in the sunlight. She couldn't believe people stepped right over it.

"Why don't people love pennies?" she asked her mommy.

"I don't know, Gracie. Maybe they don't see the value in one cent."

Gracie scooped it up. She couldn't wait to add it to her collection.

On the way home, they passed a family with a little boy about her age. They huddled under a bridge, holding a sign that read—HUNGRY PLEASE HELP.

"Mommy, why doesn't anyone help them?"

"I don't know, Gracie, maybe people just overlook them."

Gracie couldn't get the little boy out of her mind. *What was his name? Did he know Jesus? Why was his family under a bridge? Didn't they have a home?* She picked at her dinner that night, and she didn't even want ice cream!

9

Later in her bedroom, Gracie gently took the shiny penny out of her pocket. As she dropped it into her piggy bank, she thought that the people in that family were like pennies—undervalued and overlooked.

Gracie knelt by her bed with her puppy, Sofie, by her side and folded her hands. "Dear Jesus, thank you for today, and my mommy, daddy and Bubba. Thank you for Sofie, and thank you for pennies. Please let that little boy be warm and have a full tummy." She closed her prayer like she did every single night. "Please let me tell others about you one day. P.S.— Thank you for ice cream, too, Amen."

Wednesday was Gracie's favorite school day! It was chapel day, and she was excited to hear Ms. Murrill. She was explaining the verse *1 Timothy 4:12.*

"Don't let anyone look down on you because you are young, but set an example for the believers in speech, in conduct, in love, faith and purity." Ms. Murrill told the students that they were not too young to help others.

They sang Gracie's favorite song, and she hugged her teacher. "I love you, Ms. Murrill because you always teach me about Jesus."

After school, Gracie bolted through the front door.
She couldn't wait to tell her family about chapel.
"I KNOW Jesus wants me to help others. He told me!"

"What did He say? What did He sound like?" her
brother asked.

Gracie didn't have time to explain right now. She had
to create a plan!

Gracie walked with Sofie to her favorite place by the pond. Her grandma joined Gracie on the swings.

"Nini, what does Jesus sound like?"

"Sweetie, that is something you have to figure out on your own."

Gracie wrinkled her nose and said, "Well, how is he supposed to answer me if I don't know what he sounds like?"

"You will just know," Nini said with a twinkle in her eye.

Gracie thought grandmas knew everything. She was confused. Why couldn't it be as easy as putting sprinkles on ice cream? Gracie looked around the pond and noticed how all the rocks lining the edge kept the water from overflowing. A single stone couldn't do that, but all of them together could. She had her plan! Gracie jumped off her swing and ran inside.

"Daddy, Daddy, I know how to help people!"

"I knew you would come up with a plan! How?"

"My pennies aren't *my* pennies. They are from Jesus. One penny can't help anyone, but all my pennies together can!"

Gracie loved school. Well, she loved recess, snack time and Bible class. However, today Gracie couldn't wait for school to end because she was going to the bank! Her family helped her carry and push buckets of pennies into the bank. She traded them for dollars— more dollars than she could even count. She hadn't learned to count so high! The bank teller gave her a new nickname— *the penny girl.*

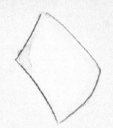

The next morning at school, Gracie asked to meet with the principal. Most second graders would be scared of that office, but she loved Principal Donna. Gracie explained how she wanted to use her pennies to help people like that little boy under the bridge. She wanted her classmates to help. She was only one little girl, but she knew that more students could help more people.

The next chapel day, Gracie and all of the students in her school gathered in the cafeteria. They prayed over the items that would be put in bags and for the people who would receive them. Students brought things like water, food, toothbrushes and soap. The best thing they added—a prayer to ask Jesus into their heart.

Gracie's friend asked, "How do I know who to give a bag to?"

Gracie replied, "If it's the right person, your heart will know." It was at that moment that Gracie finally knew what Jesus sounded like, and she would tell her family tonight.

On the way home, she passed the same bridge with the same family, and she begged her mommy to pull over. "Can we stop, pretty please—with sprinkles on top?"

"Of course, Gracie Poo, anything for you."

Gracie gave the family her Graced Pack and explained how her pennies would help them. Then she explained how Jesus loved them just like everyone else, and she prayed with them. "Dear Lord, thank you for making me and loving me enough to come to earth and die on the cross for my sins. Please forgive me for my sins. I want you to be my savior and best friend forever. Amen."

Gracie was silent on the ride home. Gracie was not usually quiet, but she was talking to Jesus. "Dear Jesus, thank you for answering my prayer and giving me a way to tell people about you."

That night at bedtime, Gracie wanted her entire family in her room-even Lamby, her stuffed lamb and her real hedgehog, Petunia. She finally knew what Jesus sounded like, and she had kept it quiet all day. She couldn't wait to share her news.

"I know how Jesus sounds! Jesus' voice is so gentle that you can't hear it; you can only feel it." Her family hugged her, and Mommy had happy tears in her eyes.

Gracie went to sleep that night knowing and wanting to share these things with the world:

1. All people are of value to Jesus.
2. All people can help others no matter their age.
3. She would help change the world one penny at a time.

CPSIA information can be obtained
at www.ICGtesting.com
Printed in the USA
BVHW062300031120
592468BV00002B/3